Wicca Book of Shadows

A Spellbook for Wiccans, Witches, and Other Magical Masters
(2022 Guide for Beginners)

Teri Hanson

PREVIOUSLY

We discussed the principles of Wicca in my first book in this Wiccan series, the essentials you need to know about starting the religion and choosing what sort of Wiccan you want to be.

This book will teach you more about spells. You will discover a variety of spells from which to pick.

Keep in your spell book.

This is a spell book, a Book of Shadows.

BEFORE WE START

MAKING A SHADOW BOOK

CHOOSING THE RIGHT BOOK

You must first pick the ideal book before you can begin creating your book of shadows. While most books of shadows are made of leather, you can make your own out of any material you desire. Be cautious, though, that any phone substance, such as fuzzy bound books, will not keep your magic. Paper notebooks and spiral bound volumes don't fare any better. Leather-bound books are said to be the best. Purchase one from your local office supply store or online.

Once you've found the notepad part, you'll have to go a bit odd. You want a notebook that speaks to you so strongly that you can feel it running through your blood. You don't want just any ordinary spiral-bound notepad. You're looking for one that speaks to you. You want to feel the energy move inside it, whether it's made of leather or organic paper. If you just choose one that does not blend well with your energy, you will discover that your spells are not as well shielded as their environment. Close your eyes and hold a few possible notebooks to your chest once you've found a few. You've discovered the correct one if you can envision yourself writing for hours in it. If you can't find it, keep looking. You want a spell book that can be handled powerfully, not a spell book packed with spells. That is a cookbook containing exclusively recipes for disasters.

WHY CHOOSING THE RIGHT BOOK IS CRITICAL?

There are evil witches in the world. They want to use your magic to make them wicked. They can corrupt your spells if they gain access to them. They will not be able to view a magic book that is in sync with your energy. Anyone who reads a book that has been enchanted by an experienced witch will see it as blank. They can only do it if the book is exclusively loyal to them.

You want a book that will stand with you. Similarly, to how the wand picks the wizard in the Harry Potter universe, the book chooses the witch in this situation. Someone will find it difficult to reverse the invisibility enchantment if you have a deep link with your book of shadows. According to legend, the only way to break another witch's spell is to spill a drop of their blood on the book (I have never attempted to take another witch's book). However, not many witches are aware of this, and it may not even be genuine. It might be an ancient wives' tale.

Another story is that the true reason a Wiccan should never let anybody touch their book. It is stated that if someone obtains another witch's book of shadows and overcomes the enchantment, that which will be able to control the true owner of the book. It nearly takes on the appearance of a voodoo doll. You'll be in the evildoer's hands until you reclaim your book.

This might all be whispering in the dark, but as they say, fiction begins with a grain of truth—better safe than sorry.

HOW TO BEGIN YOUR BOOK

To begin, a setup procedure is required. You will need to form a circle and prepare an altar.

You wish to protect your book by casting a protection spell on it. Because you are just starting, you will not be able to cast an invisibility spell; therefore, you will have to locate a decent hiding place for your book of shadows.

You will need the following items to put up the altar and circle: your selected book

The crystal that has been charged

- ❖ a pentacle an athame
- ❖ a smudge stick constructed of aspen
- ❖ beech
- ❖ blessed thistle
- ❖ fennel
- ❖ hyacinth
- ❖ pine
- ❖ walnut
- ❖ yarrow
- ❖ a candle in white
- ❖ a candle in yellow
- ❖ a candle in blue
- ❖ a single red candle
- ❖ a green candle

❖ a candle in purple

❖ a new moon

We'll go into how to create your smudge sticks in Wicca: Herbal Magic, but for now, if you can locate a pagan store, you may ask them to make you one with these components, or you can get one online. If you want to make your own, go to Wicca: Herbal Magic to learn how to do so and resume. You may have observed that a full moon is required. This is critical, and it is preferable if you can do the spell at midnight. This will offer you the most protection spell power. You want the best possible protection for your book of shadows since you don't want anyone finding it.

When you've arrived at your preferred location, set the athame, charged crystal, and pentacle on the altar surrounding the smudge stick (place your stick in a fireproof bowl.) You should also have a white candle at the back of your altar. This is critical because you should always ignite your smudge stick with a white candle. Set up the candles in a circle around the altar according to their components, with the purple candle in front of the altar on the ground. (Take care not to knock it over.) The circle should be large enough for you to easily move about your altar without upsetting the candles. Turn on the white candle. Light the matching candle as you welcome each ingredient. You should be familiar with casting a circle from the last book, so it's just a matter of understanding which candle fits with which.

- ❖ Yellow denotes air

- ❖ red denotes fire

- ❖ green denotes earth

- ❖ blue denotes water

- ❖ purple denotes spirit

After you've cast your circle, you'll want to make sure you can walk about without stepping outside of it and disrupting the magic. If necessary, move the candles to enlarge the circle. Once all of the candles have been lighted and the white candle has been replaced on the altar. It's time to summon the goddess and the horned deity. Now is the moment to enjoy the benefits of the athame. Allow two drips of blood to fall from your index finger onto the ground. No more or you risk attracting unwelcome guests. You should have a bandage on hand as well to avoid getting blood all over the place. Say this mantra while you splatter the blood on the ground.

I beseech you, Mother Goddess and Father God,

to bless this night.

Fill this circle with your defense.

Fill it to the brim with your force.

Please, grace me, as I bind my spells in a book of shadows, help me do it correctly.

Keeping it safe from those who wish to damage it makes this book a strong charm.

Thank you for joining me on this wonderful night. Please grant me the strength to bless this book and to do it well.

It's time to begin the spell when you've summoned the deities. To begin, take the charged crystal and wave it in three clockwise rounds around the book. While waving the crystal, chant.

Keep my spells safe in this vessel.

Keep it secure and in good condition.

You should repeat the chant one time for each circle you form, for a total of three times. Saying this opens the door of protection and creates a link between the magic and your book, allowing the protection spell to commence.

Light your smudge stick and, once completely lit, blow out the flame and leave it smouldering. Step away from the altar, away from the element air's candle, and place the stick in the fireproof bowl. As you take a stride into the air, recite this phrase: Mighty power, I beseech you, open this spell and help me secure my secrets and defend my thoughts.

As you travel around the circle, repeat this chant for each element. Waft the smoke over your spell book and the pentacle when you've finished using spirit. Waft it three times, then take up the pentacle and place it on the cover of the book, saying, "Protect this, oh Father and Mother, Protect this precious book."

So, I request that it be done.

After then, you may thank the deities for their assistance. Your castell your circle after you've parted ways with the deities, thanking each element as you dismiss it. Assemble your smudge stick and dispose of it in an ecologically responsible manner. You can now utilize your book of shadows to cast spells now that it has been blessed.

COMMON ERRORS REGARDING THE BOOK OF SHADOWS

Several myths are surrounding Wiccan's book of shadows. Many people think that there is a single magical book of shadows that is continuously changing and contains all of the universe's spells and answers. This is exceedingly doubtful, though, because so much power would be easy to detect, and that much power is enough to turn even the purest Wiccan—evil. Power does not become a love unless it is felt. More than likely, someone came upon a strong witch's book and mistook it for the all-powerful book.

Another common fallacy is that if you have a book of shadows, you must keep the same diary for the rest of your life. The majority of witches' books of shadows are collections of notebooks that they have filled up throughout the year. Unless you can locate a large book to keep, you will have to use more diaries than you ever imagined. This means you'll have to bless your new one every time, but don't worry, it won't take away the blessings from your other books. Many witches go through more than ten books over their lives. Make sure there are no loose papers in them; they will not be protected if they fall out of the book.

If you have an idea for a spell but don't have your book of shadows nearby, you can write it down on loose paper, but be careful to transfer it to your book of shadows, not just dump sheets of paper in it. Also, make an effort to keep your spells structured. This can range from just arranging each book with various sorts of spells to having separate volumes for various types of spells. Make a note of the dates you recorded the spells so you can track your development over time. You want a well-organized book so that when you need a spell, you can simply find it.

Many individuals believe that books of shadows are incredibly amazing and only contain finished spells. This is not correct. Many of them have half-completed spells, spells with stuff struck out and redone, and spells that make no sense. To be honest, many witches write down their theories and responses to spells in their books. These are essentially books in which you record your journey through life. If you encounter a witch with a flawless and spotless book of shadows, they have likely moved all of their previous volumes into a new book to give the impression that they know what they are doing. These people are frequently not witches, and in some cases, they are frauds. Some witches do have

OCD, which explains their virtually flawless book of shadows on occasion. "Don't trust a thin chef," as the saying goes, and you shouldn't believe a clean book of shadows either.

There is a hidden stigma that you should never let anybody see your book of shadows, and although this is somewhat correct, if you are in a coven or circle, chances are you will need to utilize it at some time. The real risk is if another witch obtains your book of shadows. That is why most witches strive to hide theirs to prevent others from using it. However, if you just take care of it, and make sure that you know where it is at all times, you can show your friends in the Wiccan community

SECTION 1

SPELLS FOR LOVE AND
RELATIONSHIPS

RELATIONSHIP SPELLS: AN OVERVIEW

There are several spells available to help you discover love and form deep ties. These spells are fantastic to have in your life since they can accomplish everything from giving you the courage to approach someone to attract the appropriate individuals into your life. There are friendship spells as well, and you may attract others to you.

This enchantment comes with a cost. You can't make someone fall in love with you; you can only influence them by fostering infatuation. You may discover that when the enchantment fades, so do their affections for you. However, if you are not careful, you may cause them to develop a strong and very deadly fixation with you. Consider if the potential negative effects are worth it. Also, attempting to compel someone to fall in love with you is a moral blunder. This can lead to major problems in some Wiccan groups. Love spells should only be used to attract the proper individuals to you or to deepen your relationship with someone you already love. If you and your partner are already in a committed relationship are both Wiccan, consider casting a love spell together. This is an excellent technique to strengthen your relationship with your lover and keep the love alive. You're not doing anything wrong, either, because casting a love spell on someone you already love won't make them fall in love with you. It invites them to fall even more in love with you than they are now.

Love spells may increase your self-esteem and make you fall in love with yourself. Because they see more than others, most Wiccans are battered down by the world. They devote more of themselves to the world than the world deserves. And ultimately, they will run out of love for themselves. This implies that they may encounter difficulties in future partnerships. A love yourself spell will reintroduce self-love into your life. When you love yourself again, it will be simpler to love people around you and offer them the encouragement they require, because you will believe the words you are uttering. To love others, you must first love yourself.

You can't also make someone your buddy. It is, however, absolutely feasible to cast a charm to attract the proper individuals into your life. People who will raise you regardless of whether they are under a spell or not.

These are the folks you will want to be friends with for the rest of your life. Friendship spells are useful since they ensure that you are befriending the proper individuals. If you don't pick someone you believe would be a wonderful buddy and instead let the great deities do their thing. You want to make friends who will benefit you rather than those who would hurt you.

There are many various sorts of love spells available, and I've included some of them in this area to help you create your book of shadows in the love section. You can add as many or as few as you like in your book of shadows, or use them to try to build your spells.

SPELLS OF LOVE

Many spells might assist you in gaining confidence in yourself. Love spells rely heavily on confidence. If you don't believe in yourself, you'll have a hard time helping others, and as a Wiccan, it's part of your moral obligation to assist people when they're in need. And, to find your real love, you must have faith in yourself.

This way, you won't miss a chance to exhibit your actual self.

These spells might also assist you in achieving clarity and serenity of mind. Some are plant spells, while others are simply spells. Some of these may be done at any time of day, night, or year, while others are more specialized. Some don't even require a circle. You can use any of the spells in this book, or you can try to make your own. Don't underestimate your abilities simply because you're starting. If you want to try a few of them first, that's OK. It's your book; it's your faith; it's who you are.

You are in command. Now that we've gained some confidence, shall we move on to the real spells?

CHARM FOR FIRST DATE CONFIDENCE

How often have you been asked on a date? If the response is not many, which may be the case because Wiccans are considered to be solitary individuals, you probably become uncomfortable on first dates, which might damage your chances of landing a second date.

First date nervousness might lead you to stammer over basic phrases or to be unable to complete simple activities successfully. Have you ever accidentally knocked anything over because you were nervous? If you freeze up in a stressful circumstance, the awkward silences might be your undoing. This is where a confidence charm might help. It should be noted that some confidence charm spells may cause problems, as they may encourage you to talk too much, boast too much, or perhaps become irritating.

You'll need one that's designed for a first date. That's where this charm comes in.

Because this is only a simple charm, you don't need anything extra. However, if you feel like you need a confidence boost on top of the charm, you may sniff some crushed borage. Keep the smells to a minimum since too much will be overpowering. Because this charm is not permanent, you should use it before your date, and if the date lasts more than an hour, you may want to "reapply." If you're not ready to tell your date about your Wiccan practices, excuse yourself to the lavatory and do it in the mirror.

What you require

- ❖ A mirror.

- ❖ a smidgeon

- ❖ crushed borage (optional)

Go to your bathroom, or any room with a mirror, right before your date. Take three nice whiffs of your borage right now. Then, in the mirror, look you in the eyes and

Three of your forces are summoned.

❖ Allow me to demonstrate my value.

❖ I'm looking for self-assurance.

❖ I am not weak; I am not meek.

Say this three times in front of the mirror, then relax and enjoy your date. If you begin to lose confidence, repeat the charm in front of a mirror. It makes no difference whether the mirror is large or little. You should do this a few times before your date to ensure that the charm is working.

SPELL FOR LOVING YOURSELF

It is critical to love oneself to choose the love you deserve. Too frequently, we select the love we believe we deserve, which is far less than the love we truly deserve. This love that we select is frequently much below what we deserve. You must love yourself enough to persuade yourself that you are deserving of greater than what is available at the time. That is the purpose of this spell. It will assist you in loving yourself so that you may discover the love you deserve.

What you'll require

- ❖ Athame
- ❖ pink candle
- ❖ charged crystal pendant

This spell is a little strange, but I've found it to be incredibly effective. You'll need to prick your finger, so carry a bandage with you so you don't wind up bleeding too much and spoiling the spell. Because this is a spell, you must do it during a moon phase. That is the phase of the new moon. This is the time to freshen and change certain aspects of your life. When you begin to love yourself, you want to feel fresh and new.

You'll also need to draw a circle around your altar. This is how you will begin your spell.

Step up to the altar once you've finished opening your circle. For this magic, you do not need to invoke the Horned God or the Mother Goddess, only the elements. However, you must still prick your finger. Place a drop of blood as near to the wick as possible on the pink candle. Allow the blood to soak into the wick before lighting the candle. Light the lamp once the majority of the blood has been absorbed. Allow it to burn for ten minutes as you think positive thoughts about yourself while looking at the flames with as little blinking as possible. You should notice yourself entering a trance-like condition. This is what you desire.

DON'T LET ANY BAD THOUGHTS GET TO YOU.
You must maintain your thoughts positive and pure for the magic to work properly. If you allow any negative ideas about yourself to enter your mind, you will have to restart the 10 minutes. When you have completed three minutes of positive thinking, blow out the candle so that it is smoldering. As you speak this mantra, wave your crystal pendant in three circles.

I am strong, pure, and bright, and I want the elements to show me that I am worthy of loving myself with a love bigger than I have ever experienced.

Say this chant in each circle. After that, put on the pendant in a necklace manner and close your eyes. Recite this spell with your dominant hand over your pendant.

- ❖ Love has both strength and might.
- ❖ This is something I'd want to have.
- ❖ Not just for others, but also myself.
- ❖ Not only do I deserve to be loved by others, but also by myself.
- ❖ I want to love myself as much as I love others.

After that, you may draw a circle around yourself. Make a point of thanking the elements.

It may seem like a self-help mantra, but this magic works miracle. It takes around two days for the full effect of the charm to take effect, but you will notice that you are smiling more often when you look in the mirror. When the effects kick in, you'll find yourself saying no to individuals who don't want to love you as much as you deserve. Learn that you must first take care of yourself before you can take care of others. And you won't feel bad about taking care of yourself.

GETTING RID OF NEGATIVE ATTACHMENTS

You most likely have persons in your life that you should not be around, making it difficult for the love yourself spell to work. As a result, you must get rid of those people from your life. Isn't it true that it's easier said than done? If they have been around for a long time, this might be incredibly difficult. Don't give up on them all at once, but if they're genuinely terrible individuals or influences, you may gradually eliminate them from your life.

Eliminate any unhealthy behaviors that may be holding you back by making you feel horrible about yourself. The only difficulty is that if you acquire them over a while, it is difficult to get rid of them overnight.

This spell will assist you in getting rid of anything harmful in your life. When you need to let go of a negative attachment, use this technique. It is not a full-fledged spell. You must smear yourself with a few items and recite a few sentences. No need for a circle.

What you'll require

❖ fireproof bowl

❖ black cohosh

❖ basil

❖ aloe

Once you've prepared a smudge stick with the items listed above, choose a peaceful spot for yourself and sit in a meditation stance. Before smudging yourself, you should sit and consider all of the toxic things you need to let go of. Gather them together into one mental "room." After that, gather your supplies and light the smudge stick. Waft the smoke about you after blowing it out until it is burning. Imagine more and more of your negativity and bad habits escaping with each wave of the smoke.

Chant this sentence again and over as you visualize all the toxins leaving your body until you feel rejuvenated.

❖ Mind, body, heart, and soul are not worth it.

❖ Allow everything to go.

When you're through, you can open your eyes and resume your daily activities. This works best during a new moon, but it may be done at any point of the lunar cycle and still be effective.

CHOOSE THE PEACE SPELL.

Peace is something that we all require in our daily lives. To become non-confrontational, we must learn to choose peace. If you are less prone to initiate a fight, you will have a better life and form stronger ties with others because you will be able to speak things out rather than yell or act irrationally.

You will be able to think more clearly if you are calm. Especially in difficult times. As a witch, it's critical that you can analyses a situation and select the appropriate spell with ease, so be calm. Because this is a spell, you will need to form a circle. However, it is not a strenuous one that necessitates any bloodletting. You don't even need any herbs for this. Know how to quickly recite a spell and how to form a circle.

Let's go right to the magic because you don't need anything else but what you need to cast a circle. You already know how to summon the elements to form a circle. After it has been cast, stand in the center and recite this spell.

❖ I am not the source of my problems.

* ❖ I am not the fury that surrounds me; instead, I choose serenity in all circumstances.

* ❖ Elements surround me, protect my intellect, and assist me in making the best choice for tranquilly every time.

You may now shut your circle after saying this spell. Say the spell as many times as you believe necessary before closing your circle.

FRIENDSHIP IS ALSO IMPORTANT.

Many individuals do not associate friendship with love. These folks fail to see that no one can love you as deeply as your best buddy. There isn't even a significant other. It is essential to have friends that care about and love you, just as it is essential for you to love yourself.

You want pals who are concerned about your well-being. These buddies frequently tell you what you need to hear rather than what you want to hear. For example, if they say that individual isn't right for you, continue with care. These folks are difficult to find. To be completely whole, you must have friendship in your life. You don't need many friends, but you do need one or two good ones. People who will motivate you to be yourself rather than someone else. You should make friends who you wish to accompany you on your journey here on Earth. These buddies will be there for you throughout your journey here, from meeting the person of your dreams to walking down the aisle. And twenty years from now, you'll grin as you remember all the good moments you had and how close you are.

There are several friendship spells; I'll focus on the most frequent and popular spells.

SPELL FOR MAKING NEW FRIENDS

Sometimes we look about and discover that those we thought where friends were not genuinely friends, or that we have drifted apart from friends, and we realize we need new relationships—long-term ties.

Wiccans are often introverted and have a difficult time interacting with others. This spell differs slightly from the others we've discussed, but not much.

- ❖ You'll need ribbon or yarn (enough to make a bracelet)
- ❖ a candle in yellow
- ❖ oil of fortune

To begin, gather your materials and form a circle. Before lighting the candle, dab a drop of the oil on it to anoint it. Begin braiding the yarn into a friendship bracelet. Say this spell while braiding your hair.

INTERTWINED AND WEAVED

May our relationship not be shattered, closest friends, draw to me so that I will so that it must be

Rep this spell until you've completed your bracelet. Then, add three drops of the oil to the bracelet and wrap them around the candle until it burns out. When the candle has burned out, put on the bracelet. Finally, draw a circle around yourself and thank each element as it leaves.

SPIRITUAL CONNECTION CHARM

Because this is a chant rather than a spell, you do not need to cast a circle. You are just sending out positive ideas into the atmosphere to make a profound spiritual connection with someone. These persons might be friends or family members. Spiritual relationships are essential since you require someone who enlightens your spirit.

Go into a secluded room and shut yourself away when you have the time. Close your eyes and think about the form of relationship you want. Keep in mind that you want to locate something deep within your hobbies. While you're picturing, recite this mantra to the link.

Come to my heart, my soul, my spiritual companion, and I will welcome you in.

Repeat the mantra three times before opening your eyes. You have finished the chant. Now get out there and start talking to folks. Soon, you'll meet someone who ignites your very spirit. Be prepared to go out there and locate the individual. This spell will also play a role in attracting you to the proper individuals. Apple

Divination Spell Divination is an exccllent method for determining the genuine intentions of persons around you. It may also be used to find love.

Divination might assist you in finding real love or friendship. I know the Harry Potter universe mocked divination by casting a mad lady as the professor who taught it.

It is, however, a true spell that should be regarded seriously.

What you'll require

- ❖ an apple fruits
- ❖ apple peel

❖ A saucepan of hot water that is on the stove.

To begin, peel an apple in a spiral manner in a circular motion. Say this mantra while you peel.

Please, apple peel let us play a game in which you take the first initial of my real friend's first name.

The enigmas of love and the joys of Halloween

Make your sign obvious to me with the assistance of Pomona.

After you've finished the chant, hurl the peel into the ocean over your shoulder (this may take some practice). The peel will then unfold as it warms up; forming the shape of the first letter of the first name of the person you're looking for.

ROMANCE AND LOVE

Finally, the portion you've been looking forward to. True love spells. Everyone desires and is entitled to find their true love. These spells can assist you in attracting the love you deserve. However, if you employ these spells with incorrect motives, they may not always have the best consequences. If you want to attract genuine love, not the love you believe you desire, you must have noble intentions. As previously said, you cannot compel someone to fall in love with you, and attempting to do so can be devastating.

Allow just the appropriate person to fall in love with you. If you don't, you'll be following someone for years and losing out on the proper person—talk about squandering time.

ATTRACTION CHARM OF HIGH QUALITY

You'd like to attract a high-quality connection. The better you connect and the closer you are to pure love, the higher the quality of your connection.

This charm entails a talisman in the form of perfume or cologne.

What you'll require

- ❖ carnation oil
- ❖ favorite perfume or fragrance

To utilize this charm, put a few drops of carnation oil into a bottle of your favorite eau de toilette. This will draw only pure love to you. Say this chant once you've added the oil.

Love of excellence, as I will thus mote it brings me

That's all there is to it for this one. Whenever you walk out, spritz yourself with the enchanted spray and watch it work its magic. You'll find someone worth being in a relationship with shortly.

SMUDGE ROMANCE ATTRACTION

Everyone wishes for romance in their lives. Romance is what sustains love. If you desire romance in your life, this smudge will assist you in attracting it.

What you'll require

- ❖ chickweed apple carnation

- ❖ cinnamon chili

- ❖ Wallflower in violet

- ❖ a candle in white

- ❖ a fire-resistant bow

Make or purchase a smudge stick using these components (minus the white candle) When you have a When the smudge stick has completely dried; it is time to begin the ceremony.

Light the white candle and place the smudge stick on it. Blow out the fire on the stick and place it in a container a fire-resistant bowl Waft smoke over yourself and repeat this incantation.

❖ Passionate light

❖ Build my fire

❖ Infuse passion into my partnership

After saying the mantra four or five times and thoroughly smudging oneself, you can throw out and remove the smudge stick. Have fun romancing!

BATH RITUAL FOR A BLIND DATE

This magic is a little unusual. This entails taking a bath. You must, however, draw a circle. Not at all Be concerned about being nude in the presence of the goddess, as it is normal in Wiccan tradition not to be shielded You are free to be yourself. You should concentrate on relaxing and unwinding throughout this bath allowing all of your stress to leave your body You want to be revitalized and regenerated so that optimism may flow freely gushing through you.

Because this is a blind date, you should be more aware of your inner sentiments. This is critical since you are completely unfamiliar with the individual If there is something strange about them, you should be cautious being able to flee before you are in danger Then you want to be safe. Be cautious, but not overly so. Concerned. You want to exude confidence and strength. That is the purpose of this bath. It will provide you with security. You need clarity and confidence to make this date a successor to bail out before things go wrong.

What you'll require

- ❖ bathtub

- ❖ bringing the water to temperature

- ❖ petals of roses

- ❖ chamomile

- ❖ iris with a blue flag

- ❖ cinnamon essential oil

- ❖ centaury

- ❖ basil

- ❖ a light blue candle

- ❖ a single red candle

- ❖ a candle in yellow

  - ❖ candle in purple

Because you're in a tub, you don't have to burn

the candles in a circle around yourself in this

ceremony hard. Make a candle circle beside the tub. Fill your bath with water that is the temperature you want until it is at a comfortable height for you. Combine the rose petals, chamomile, blue flag iris, and basil in a mixing bowl your drinking water Before lighting the candles and opening your circle, anoint them with cinnamon oil, Cinnamon is an irritant, so add it to your bath) Get into your bath and unwind. Feel the benefits of all of the plants in the bath. Now is the time when you cleanse yourself and prepare for the approaching date it is ideal to do this as near to your home as possible. Date as soon as possible, so that the benefits don't wear off. It lasts around twenty-four hours. If you do this, the you should be alright the morning of your date after you've done your bath (take your time letting the water cool); you may shut your circle and get back to your day.

SECTION 2

SPELLS FOR WEALTH AND PROSPERITY

WEALTH AND PROSPERITY SPELLS: AN OVERVIEW

We all require some riches and prosperity in our life, and that's just OK. There are times when we are a bit short on cash, and there is nothing wrong with requesting a little assistance. This is very natural, and there are even spells available to assist you in becoming successful in your business and money-making pursuits. With the help of these charms, you may find yourself with a bit more money than you believed possible.

I must caution you, though, not to be greedy. While wealth is one thing, you should not try to generate money with spells if you are unwilling to put in the work. These spells should only be used to supplement your current income. You should also avoid hoarding your earnings. Prosperity is only fully noticed when it is shared. Help the little old lady down the street grow a more successful garden, and offer the next-door neighbor a small monetary gift to help with Christmas. It doesn't have to be much; just spread the love.

That being said, there are a few spells that can be used without making you hungry. They replenish your crops and your piggy bank to assist you in becoming more prosperous.

These spells will assist you in locating coins and other little amounts of money that are lying about. If you do chance to locate larger bills, your belief and power will be stronger than that of most novices. However, if you know who the money belongs to, you should undoubtedly return it. If no one is nearby, that money was meant for you.

SPELLS OF SUCCESS AND PROSPERITY

These charms are about achieving success and prospering in your activities. These may not always provide you with random bursts of money, but they do open the door to producing the money you require and ensuring your success in your garden and companies.

Everyone wants to be successful in what they do, and these spells will help you get there. They will not, however, keep you on the success ladder indefinitely; you must buck up and put in the work to remain successful. You can't expect magic to perform all of your jobs for you.

SPELL FOR GARDEN PLANTING

If you're a gardener, you probably want your crops to thrive and be plentiful. This spell can assist with that. This charm should be cast when you are planting your garden to ensure its success from the moment the seeds are planted. This spell is a little different from the others we've posted so far, but it's an excellent one that many witches have shared.

What you'll require

- ❖ For each row of your garden

- ❖ Use two wooden posts.

- ❖ 1 pastel ribbon piece for each stake

- ❖ fresh leaves on a tiny tree or shrub branch

- ❖ Seeds or plants in a 2 qt.

- ❖ container

- ❖ 1-quart milk

- ❖ 12 cup honey

Pour the milk and honey mixture into the container. Insert the branch, leaves down, into the container. Remove all of the materials to the outside. As you begin a row of seeds or plants, place a stake in the ground and tie a piece of ribbon to it. Say this phrase when you tie the ribbon on.

With this flawless love, I offer you, sprout and bloom with life afresh.

When you finish a row, repeat the stake/ribbon/chant procedure and carry on with the next row. You should repeat the chant twice for each row you perform, once for each stake with the ribbon you place in the ground.

After you've finished planting your garden, take the milk mixture and return to the first row. While chanting this spell,

❖ Take the branch and sprinkle the concoction throughout each row.

❖ Throughout, milk and honey flow.

❖ Fertilize and sprout each seed

❖ Garden sprites, dancing, and a

❖ Every day, I twirl and giggle in my garden.

❖ Bring a lot of development and abundance to this location.

❖ You dance, play, and stroll everywhere you go.

❖ After that, water and care for your garden regularly.

❖ Jar of Honey Abundance

When you think about it, this is an odd ritual, yet it truly works. It began as a hoodoo ceremony and has now moved to the Wiccan culture due to its success.

The honey abundance jar is a great method to bring riches into your life. If you do this, you will see that things improve over time.

What you'll require

- ❖ a pinch of chamomile

- ❖ honey

- ❖ a pinch of Irish moss

- ❖ a hinge-top jar

- ❖ a sprinkle of cinnamon

- ❖ money

- ❖ a little piece of paper

- ❖ a pen

- ❖ a small green candle

- ❖ matches

To begin, make a list of what you're looking for. Is it new employment or a second source of income? When you're writing, make sure your pen never leaves the paper. Drag the pen across even if you're starting a new word.

CONTINUITY IS ESSENTIAL IN THIS SITUATION.

After that, you place the paper in the jar. Cover the paper with leaves and drizzle with honey.

CLOSE AND SECURE THE JAR'S LID.

You now rub the money oil into your candle before lighting it. Allow a few drops of wax to drip onto the jar's lid, then use that wax to bind the candle to the lid. Then, extinguish the candle fully in one shot. Repeat this technique once a month and you'll be astonished at how much of a difference it makes.

PROSPERITY SPELL IN THE MOONLIGHT

This money magic should be performed at the full moon to maximize the spell's potency.

You'll want to do it when the moon is at its fullest, which means staying up late. Most Wiccans are night owls, so that shouldn't be a problem.

What you'll require

- ❖ full moon

- ❖ cauldron

- ❖ water

- ❖ silver coin

Cast a circle around your cauldron once everything is ready. After you've formed your circle, pour the water into your cauldron until it's half-filled. After that, drop the silver coin into the water. Say this chant three times while waving your hands over the water, as if attempting to scoop up the silver of the moon's reflections.

My appeal was heard by the Moon Goddess.

Bring me luck on this night.

Let me use it wisely and well to retain that prosperity for the rest of my life.

After you've completed this, you can shut your circle and pack your belongings.

CHARM FOR INTERVIEW SUCCESS

This is easy and does not need the use of a chant.

- ❖ green candle

- ❖ physical snapshot of oneself

- ❖ paperclip

- ❖ $1 bill

Light the candle, then take the dollar note and wave it in front of the flame on both sides. After that, extinguish the flame and paperclip the money to the portrait of yourself. Bring this with you to your interview in your handbag or wallet.

CHARM FOR BUSINESS SUCCESS

This is also a pretty simple charm to do; however, it does require some talking.

What you'll require

❖ a silver jingle bell strand

Keep the bells ringing and speak

All year long, the sound of the bells brings me good fortune and tremendous success.

Hang the bells on your business's door, and every time they ring, it will bring you success.

MONEY ATTRACTING FACTORS

Money Charm with Cinnamon

This spell is designed to bring you just money. The money may not be large, but it should give you a lift.

What you'll require

❖ cinnamon powder

❖ belief

❖ dollar bill

This spell must be performed on a Thursday since this is the most powerful day of the week for money spells. Using a small amount of water, wet both sides of the $1 bill. After that, moisten your finger and dip it in the cinnamon.

Make three lines with the cinnamon on a dollar note and place it where you regularly store your money. Be sure to trust that this works and then watch the money come in.

PYRITE AS A PROSPERITY STONE

This is a unique sort of magic. Crystal magic, to be precise. Crystal magic is the technique of combining crystals to achieve the desired effect. Pyrite is used in this charm to attract money.

Other crystals attract money, but Pyrite is the most powerful.

Crystal magic is simple, but it does require trust to be successful. You must first charge your crystals with the information you wish to receive from them. You'll see in the preceding spells that you'll need to charge a clear quartz crystal to perform the spell. There was, however, no guidance on how to charge a crystal. A guide is required. To charge a crystal, first, hold it tightly in your palm and "make a wish." Your wish can be anything; however certain crystals work well with other crystals. Citrine, green aventurine, tiger's eye, moss agate, ruby, jade, and pyrite are the greatest stones for riches and success. To use a crystal, just make a wish while holding it tightly with your eyes closed and leaving it in the light of a full moon overnight.

They are ready after they have been charged. Keep in mind that the charges, even if unused, do not last forever and must be refreshed once a month at the full moon. Charging a variety of crystals is usually a smart idea. If you don't have a specific desire for your crystals and only want to charge them for future spells, place them in the light of the full moon and they will charge with a neutral power.

You can charge as many or as few crystals as you like, but the more you charge, the more prepared you will be in the future. Every full moon, I usually have ten to twelve crystals charging.

What you'll require

- ❖ one pyrite crystal
- ❖ eight more riches crystals of your choosing believe

Start by charging your crystals during a full moon. Arrange them in a circle with pyrite in the center once they've been charged. Place these crystals in a high-traffic location of your property. As an example, consider a high shelf in your living room or bedroom. The stones will work their magic on your house, and you will be showered with prosperity in no time. Make sure the crystals remain upright regularly. You want to get the most out of your crystals, and if any of them have broken formation, they will cause problems in the magical stream.

Here are some money rituals and charms to bring you money and wealth. Remember not to be greedy and to share your prosperity with others.

SECTION 3

SPELLS FOR HEALTH AND WELL-BEING

INTRODUCTION TO SPELLS FOR HEALTH AND WELL-BEING

Everyone desires to be well and to live a happy, healthy life. Life, however, has other intentions. These spells are evergreen, since sickness, injury, and death all attempt to creep up on you. Health and well-being spells keep you healthy in general. You can't fix a shattered bone or a sprained spleen, but you can prevent the flu and treat minor injuries.

I must tell you that you cannot resurrect someone who has died. Cannot. Can't. Can't. Can't. Some of history's greatest witches have gone insane trying. The world's most famous alchemist, Nicholas Flame, became insane because he produced a stone to raise the dead, and the effects drove him insane. You've undoubtedly heard that name before, if not in the Harry Potter universe, then in the first novel, Harry Potter and the Sorcerer's Stone. The Philosopher's Stone was claimed to keep the person who held it alive for as long as they held the stone. What the book didn't say was that the stone might potentially bring the dead back to life. However, when this was stated in the Deathly Hallows, Ian several, the recipient of the resurrection stone, went insane.

Keep that in mind—just a heads-up. Moving forward, only utilize healing spells for their intended purpose. Heal minor wounds. There is no magical elixir that can regrow or cure damaged bones in a single night, nor is there a means to restore an organ. Attempting to do so might have disastrous consequences.

There are no true injury healing spells in this area because healing spells are at a level higher than a novice. They need a lot of energy and may be devastating if not done correctly, so store them until you have more experience with higher-level spells. There are spells in this area that deal with personal health and well-being. For example, security and mental wellness.

HEALTH QUICK RECOVERY BATH

If you've been hurt or aren't feeling well, you probably want to go back to normalcy as soon as possible. This spell will hasten your healing and get you back on your feet sooner. It is not an instant healing spell, but it will hasten the process.

What you'll require

- ❖ angelica

- ❖ arnica

- ❖ chamomile yellow candle

- ❖ castor oil

- ❖ candle in purple

- ❖ bathwater to your preferred temperature

To begin, fill the tub with water to the temperature you choose and at a water level that is comfortable for you. Add angelica, arnica, and chamomile (as much as you think you need).

Allow the herbs to soak in the water for a few minutes.

While they're doing that, anoint and ignite the candles with castor oil. Turn off the lights and jump into the bath, soaking until the water cools. Allow your thoughts to relax and float away to your happy spot while you soak. Consider your body to be entire, with nothing wrong with it. After you get out of the bath, extinguish the candles and go about your business.

ANXIETY RELIEVING SPELL

Anxiety is a prevalent issue among Wiccans. This is because they have empathic sensitivity. If you have an anxiety attack, you can use this charm to help you. Anxiety may strike at any time; thus, this spell is designed to have all of the benefits of an anxiety spell without requiring a large number of materials. All you need is a few moments of silence.

Find a peaceful area to do this ritual; if you are in public and can't wait, the toilet should suffice. Curl up into a meditation stance as near to the floor as you can. Take three deep breaths and repeat this mantra three times.

- ❖ Anxiety,

- ❖ Please take your leave and go from me.

Repeat the chorus ten times. Watch as your fear fades and you discover that you can have fun even in the most crowded of settings.

INFUSION OF YELLOW SPELL TO PICK ME UP

Everyone needs a pick-me-up spell, and this one make use of the color yellow, which is a proven mood enhancer.

What you'll require

- ❖ a candle in yellow

- ❖ ribbon in yellow (enough for a bracelet)

- ❖ paper in yellow (very small piece)

- ❖ Marker in yellow

- ❖ the oil of castor

To begin, anoint the candle with castor oil and allow it to soak in. While the oil is setting, grab a yellow marker and write on a piece of yellow paper how you want to feel. Use cursive when you want to feel pleased, thrilled, or joyful, and don't take the marker from the paper until you're finished. After you've put down the word, weave the ribbons together to construct your bracelet. Say this magic when you braid your hair.

Take my attitude, raise me, and help me feel better soon with this little bracelet so skillfully crafted braided by hand by me.

Say this as many times as it takes to braid the bracelet. Set the bracelet aside once you've finished braiding it. Bring out the candle and light it. Place the paper in the flame and let it burn. When the paper has completely burned, take the bracelet and blow out the candle. Then, while holding the bracelet in the smoke, wait for it to evaporate. Put on the bracelet and notice how your mood improves.

RED JASPER IS SAID TO PROVIDE ENERGY AND ENDURANCE.

Life necessitates the use of energy and endurance. This is especially true if you are an active person. This spell will assist you in maintaining your energy and completing chores that you have been wanting to complete but never seem to have the time or energy to perform at the end of the day. It might also help you complete that marathon that you signed up for. This spell will help you with anything that demands energy.

This spell necessitates the usage of chakras. You must first find your base (root) chakra, which is located at the base of your spine—a fast wcb search can help you with this.

What you need

- ❖ a tad of chakra knowledge
- ❖ red jasper stone

Begin by locating your root chakra. For this to work, you must be completely calm. Place the red jasper stone on your root chakra and visualize the energy flowing through you. Cast this magic.

Spare me some energy stones to fill me up and make me run.

After that, rest for fifteen minutes with the stone on your chakra. Repeat the process twice more.

You can resume your day when the third time's rest interval has ended.

SPELLS OF GOOD HEALTH

Collar for Pet Security

If you have pets, you most certainly wish to protect them. But what if you aren't there to defend them? We can't be at home every minute of every day to keep an eye on them. That is the purpose of this spell. This spell will get attached to your dog's collar. It's essentially a collar smeared with protecting herbs.

What you'll require

- ❖ pet collar
- ❖ angelica

- ❖ blessed thistle

- ❖ basil

- ❖ bay

To begin, obtain a smudge stick made from the four plants listed above. You've heard the story before.

Find a peaceful place, ignite the stick, and then blow it out to as you do not, however, want to put it in a dish. The ashes from the stick should fall on the collar. Several times, wave the smudge stick over the collar while saying,

- ❖ "Mother Goddess,

- ❖ Guard my companion against all evil till the end."

Continue saying this until the smudge stick is well over halfway down. After that, you may remove the stick and massage the ashes into the collar. Clean up your messes, and then leave the collar overnight with the ashes rubbed into it. Wash and dry the collar before putting it on your pet. The collar will now offer your pet the necessary protection.

HOME PROTECTION WITH A WITCH BOTTLE

This bit of magic will create a protective zone around your home, ensuring that terrible things do not happen while you are away.

What you'll require

- ❖ a depleted wine bottles

- ❖ a little blue taper candle

❖ cat's eye stone (small)

❖ blessed thistle

❖ paper

❖ Pen

To begin, grab the bottle and thoroughly clean it. Check to see whether it is clean. Once the bottle is clean, take a piece of paper and a pen and writes down what you want from the jar (protection of the household 80 is a good place to start). Make certain that once you begin writing, the pen does not leave the paper until you have completed it.

Insert the paper into the bottle and top with the blessed thistle and cat's eye stone. Re-cork the bottle and ignite the candle. Apply a few droplets of wax on the cork to secure the candle, and then let it burn out. When the candle has burned out, place the bottle in your living room to safeguard the entire house. This should be done once a month.

MORNING BOOSTER POTION

If you're anything like me, getting out of bed in the morning is difficult, and coffee doesn't always help. This potion, on the other hand, has the potential to work.

What you'll require

❖ coffee

❖ aloe Vera (1 tsp. per 12 cups)

❖ Cayenne pepper (only a pinch!)

❖ A century (less than a tsp.)

Make it every morning, just like normal coffee,

and watch the motivation kick in.

MISCELLANEOUS SPELLS

INTRODUCTION TO VARIOUS SPELLS

Many additional spells are beneficial in everyday life but do not fall into a specific category of spells. These spells vary from simple to complex. We will simply cover the fundamentals in this book. As you gain experience, you will be able to cast increasingly challenging spells. In the following book, there will be more challenging spells. Herbal Magic in Wicca.

Spells

New Year's Elemental Blessing

This is magic to bring you good fortune in the New Year.

What you'll require

- ❖ Water

- ❖ Athame

- ❖ cauldron

Cast a circle, and then stand at the altar with your pot. Fill the cauldron halfway with water. Prick your finger with your athame. Do not apply a bandage to your finger. Dip your pierced finger in the water and swirl it around. Cast this magic.

- ❖ See my new year,

- ❖ Blessed One in the Sky.

- ❖ Give me prosperity,

- ❖ Take away my dread,

- ❖ and make it magnificent,

- ❖ oh, lovely God.

Close your circle and express gratitude to the elements.

SPELL OF CLARITY

This spell will help you to cleanse your thoughts and gain clarity.

Form a circle and recite this chant.

- ❖ Brain on fire

- ❖ with questions alright

- ❖ Clear your mind and

- ❖ Get it corrected.

Close your circle and express gratitude to the elements.

AVOCADO BEAUTY CURE

This is magic that will brighten your skin and bring out your inner beauty 84.

What you'll require

- ❖ chamomile
- ❖ avocado

Combine the two ingredients and apply them to your face. Allow for thirty minutes of resting time. Say this spell before you remove something.

- ❖ The beauty within,
- ❖ Beauty without,
- ❖ Clean my skin,
- ❖ Don't make me scream,

❖ Make me bright,

❖ Shining,

❖ And new as I beg of you

Remove the mixture from your face and thoroughly cleanse it.

www.ingramcontent.com/pod-product-compliance
Lightning Source LLC
LaVergne TN
LVHW050846200726
843507LV00001B/454